MIGHTY MOUNTAINS

by Noah Leatherland

Minneapolis, Minnesota

Credits
Images are courtesy of Shutterstock.com. With thanks to Getty Images, Thinkstock Photo, and iStockphoto. Cover – Olga Danylenko, Gleb Tarro. Recurring – hugolacasse, donatas1205. 2–3 – Technicsorn Stocker. 4–5 – Jeanette Virginia Goh, Grey Zone. 6–7 – DariaGa, EB Adventure Photography. 8–9 – Peter Hermes Furian, Designua, frentusha. 10–11 – Vixit, Md Robiul Islam Idris. 12–13 – Taras Kushnir, Linas D. 14–15 – Marcus Placidus, Anastasia Mazureva. 16–17 – Ravi Chip, Thomas Dekiere. 18–19 – emerald_media, Saulius Damulevicius. 20–21 – Yankovsky88, Salienko Evgenii. 22–23 – A_B_C, SIHASAKPRACHUM.

Bearport Publishing Company Product Development Team
Publisher: Jen Jenson; Director of Product Development: Spencer Brinker; Editorial Director: Allison Juda; Editor: Cole Nelson; Editor: Tiana Tran; Production Editor: Naomi Reich; Art Director: Kim Jones; Designer: Kayla Eggert; Designer: Steve Scheluchin; Production Specialist: Owen Hamlin

Library of Congress Cataloging-in-Publication Data is available at www.loc.gov or upon request from the publisher.

ISBN: 979-8-89577-080-1 (hardcover)
ISBN: 979-8-89577-527-1 (paperback)
ISBN: 979-8-89577-197-6 (ebook)

© 2026 BookLife Publishing
This edition is published by arrangement with BookLife Publishing.

North American adaptations © 2026 Bearport Publishing Company. All rights reserved. No part of this publication may be reproduced in whole or in part, stored in any retrieval system, or transmitted in any form or by any means, electronic, mechanical, photocopying, recording, or otherwise, without written permission from the publisher. Bearport Publishing is a division of FlutterBee Education Group.

For more information, write to Bearport Publishing, 3500 American Blvd W, Suite 150, Bloomington, MN 55431.

CONTENTS

Our Home 4

Mountains. 6

Pushing Plates 8

Mountain Parts. 10

Mountaineers 12

Avalanches 14

Landslides. .16

Altitude 18

Gearing Up 20

Safe Studies 22

Glossary. 24

Index 24

OUR HOME

Check out our home planet, Earth! It has everything we need to live. However, not everything on Earth is very nice. . . .

Earth can sometimes be a dangerous place. Some things on our planet can **damage** land and buildings. Others can even cause death!

A tornado

LET'S LEARN ABOUT MIGHTY MOUNTAINS!

MOUNTAINS

What are mountains? They are tall, rocky **landforms**. Mountains often have **steep** sides.

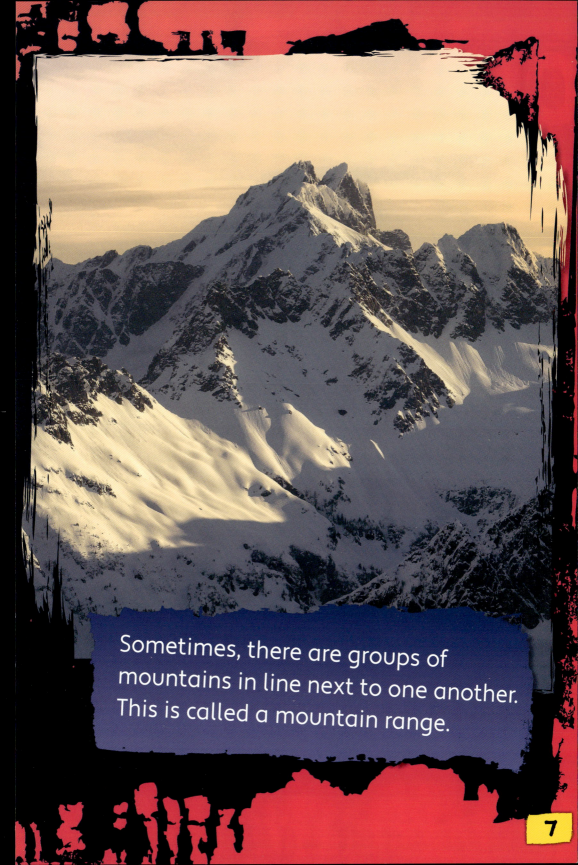

Sometimes, there are groups of mountains in line next to one another. This is called a mountain range.

PUSHING PLATES

How do mountains form? Earth has four different layers. The top layer is the crust. It is made of huge, flat rocks called plates.

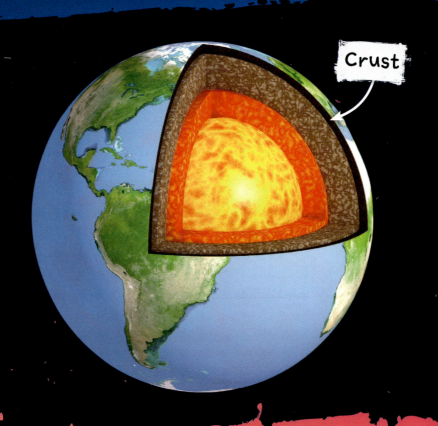

Crust

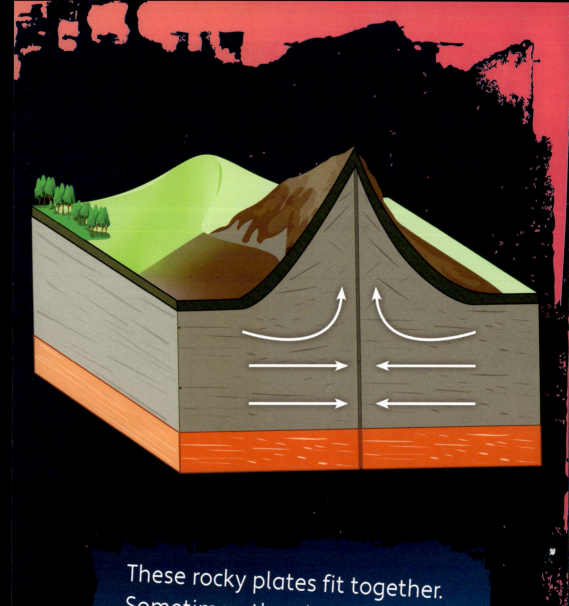

These rocky plates fit together. Sometimes, the plates push against each other. This forces rock upward to create mountains.

MOUNTAIN PARTS

Summit

A mountain's bottom is often referred to as the base. Meanwhile, the top of a mountain is its summit.

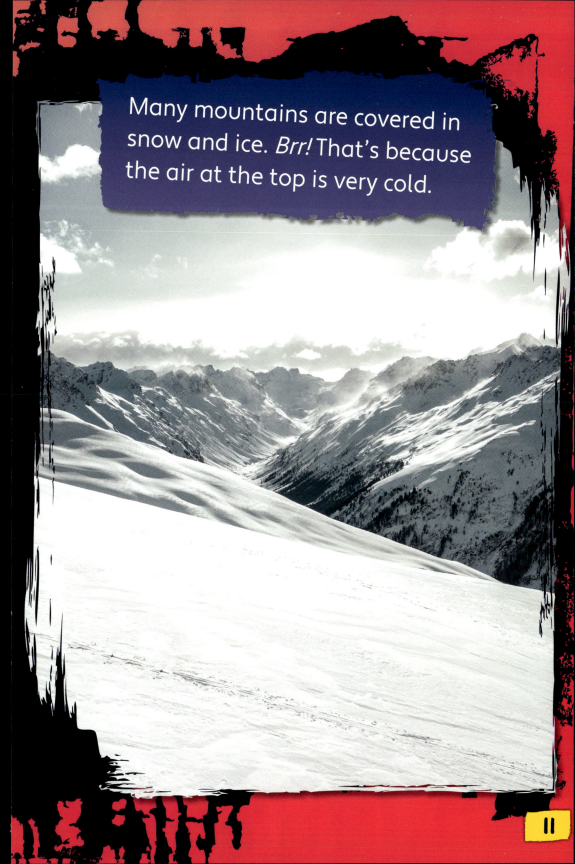

Many mountains are covered in snow and ice. *Brr!* That's because the air at the top is very cold.

MOUNTAINEERS

Reaching the summit can be very hard. However, some people like the challenge. They are called mountaineers.

These climbers must face a lot of dangers. They could get stuck, fall, or even **freeze**!

AVALANCHES

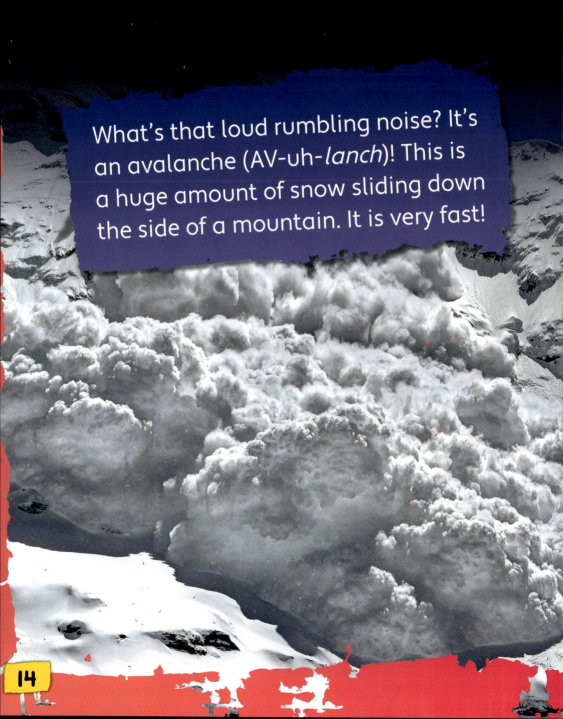

What's that loud rumbling noise? It's an avalanche (AV-uh-*lanch*)! This is a huge amount of snow sliding down the side of a mountain. It is very fast!

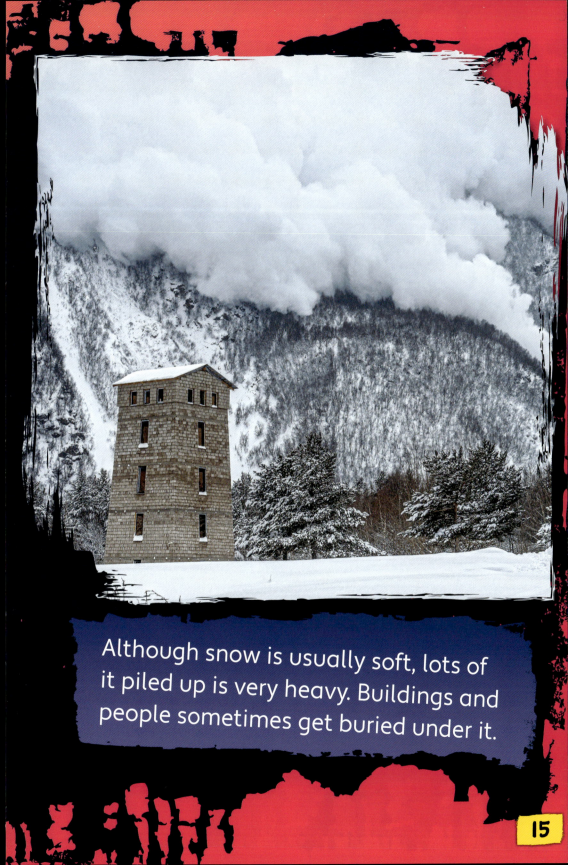

Although snow is usually soft, lots of it piled up is very heavy. Buildings and people sometimes get buried under it.

LANDSLIDES

Snow is not the only thing that can tumble down a mountain. Rocks and soil can slip, too!

When large amounts of rock fall down a mountain, it is called a landslide. This can damage homes and block roads.

ALTITUDE

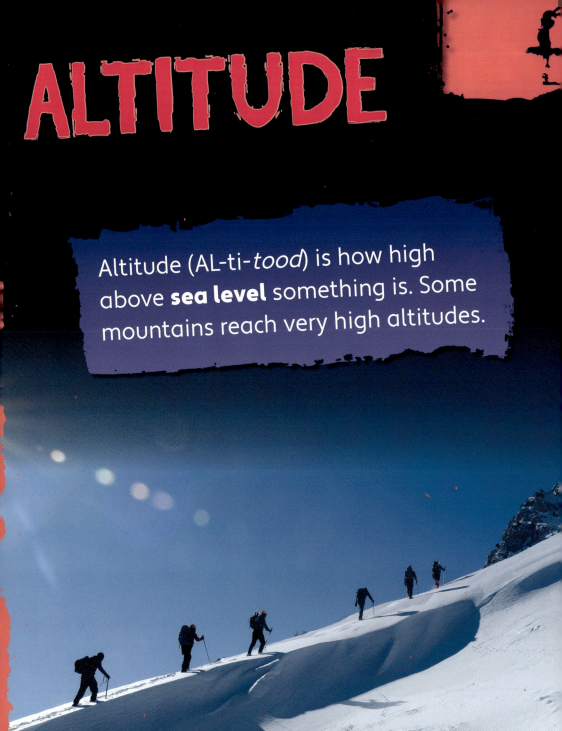

Altitude (AL-ti-*tood*) is how high above **sea level** something is. Some mountains reach very high altitudes.

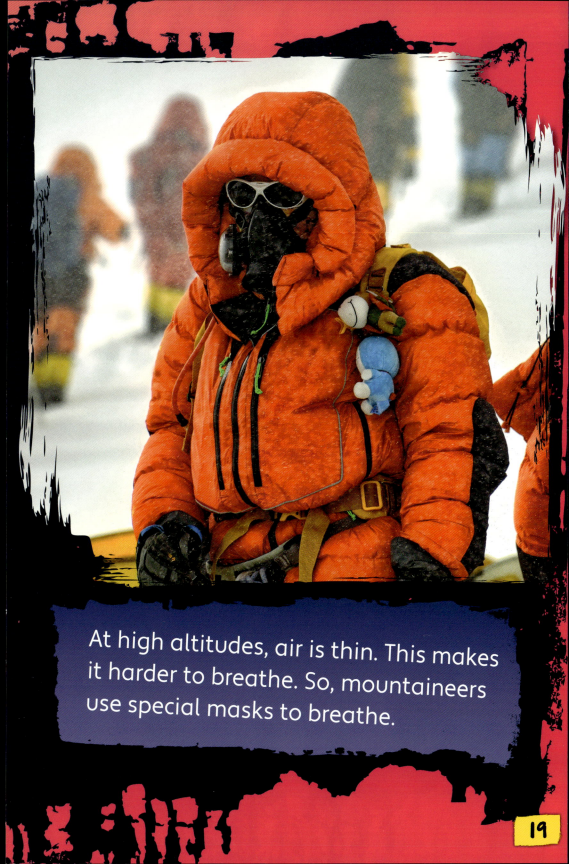

At high altitudes, air is thin. This makes it harder to breathe. So, mountaineers use special masks to breathe.

GEARING UP

Masks aren't the only special gear that mountaineers use. Crampons are spikes that attach to shoes. These help climbers **grip** ice and snow.

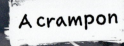
A crampon

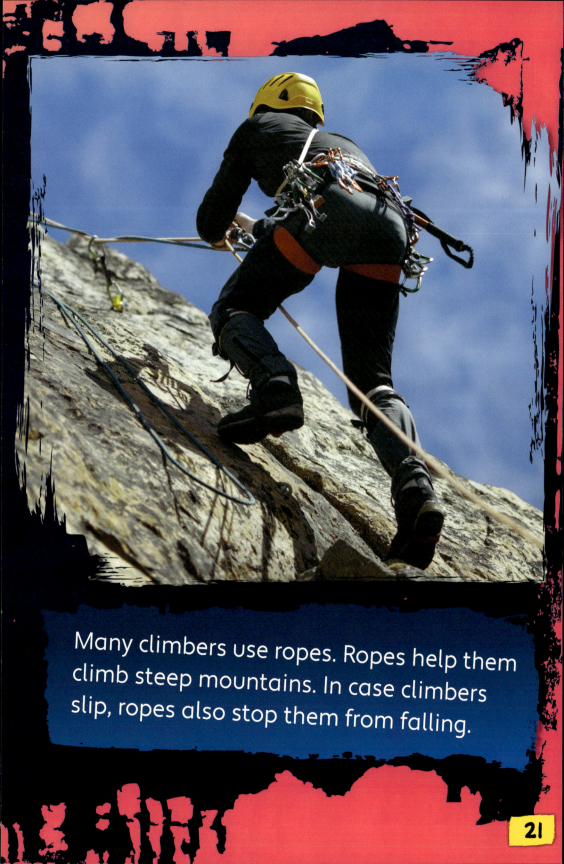

Many climbers use ropes. Ropes help them climb steep mountains. In case climbers slip, ropes also stop them from falling.

SAFE STUDIES

Mountains are beautiful and super interesting to learn about. However, they can still be dangerous.

Leave climbing mountains to the **experts**. They know the best ways to reach summits while staying safe.

GLOSSARY

damage harm

experts people who know a lot about a subject

freeze to become cold enough that liquids become solids

grip a strong hold on something

landforms natural features on Earth's surface

sea level the height of the ocean's surface, often used to compare measurements above this point

steep something that goes almost straight up

INDEX

air 11, 19
ice 11, 20
land 5
masks 19–20
mountaineers 12, 19–20
plates 8–9
rocks 6, 8–9, 16–17
rope 21
snow 11, 14–16, 20
summits 10, 12, 23